DISPLACED REFLECTIONS

DISPLACED REFLECTIONS

Refugees and displaced people from Burma shed light on
life, love, and faith.

By Oddny Gumaer
Photos by Brent Madison

PARTNERS
Publishing House

Displaced Reflections: Refugees and displaced people from Burma shed light on life, love, and faith

Copyright © 2007 by Oddny Gumaer
ISBN: 0-9777706-0-5

Requests for information should be addressed to:
Partners Publishing House®, the publishing group of Partners Relief and Development®
P.O. Box 27220, Albuquerque, NM 87125, USA
www.partnersworld.org

Author: Oddny Gumaer
Photos: Brent Madison unless otherwise noted
Graphic Design: Oddny Gumaer

Printed in Thailand by actsco.org

For the displaced people of Burma

All the income from this book will
go to help them.

"I shall no longer ask myself if this or that is expedient, but only if it is right. I shall do this, not because I am noble or unselfish, but because life slips away, and because I need for the rest of my journey a star that will not play false to me, a compass that will not lie.

I shall do this, because I cannot find it in me to do anything else. I am lost when I balance this against that, I am lost when I ask if this is safe, I am lost when I ask if men will approve. Therefore I shall try to do what is right, and to speak what is true."

Alan Paton, *Cry The Beloved Country*

LEARNING TO CARE

So there we were on the bed of an old pickup truck together with some other passengers who looked like they had just walked out of National Geographic Magazine.

Their faces were so full of wrinkles that a street map of New York City would have looked boring in comparison. They were looking at us with a mixture of curiosity, fear and astonishment. "Look at those big feet and the long noses," they were probably thinking. "How ugly their clothes are. No color, no ornaments. Is that a man or a woman? It has short hair and long pants. But it appears to have breasts."

We glanced at their big smiles. The smiles were genuine, but why were their teeth black and their gums purple? Their costumes were so colorful. Hot pink seemed to be the color of the year. It was mixed with some red, purple, blue and black in intricate patterns that got an added dimension of beauty from the seeds and shells that were sewn into the cloth. Around their necks were multicolored glass bead necklaces. Some time ago they must have found towels at the market and understood their true purpose, which of course was to be used as turbans. Now most of the Karen wore them in different hues that perfectly matched the rest of their outfits.

Sitting like that in an old truck that has been converted to a primitive bus, riding on roads that had just recently only seen elephants walking on them, provided time to reflect. That is exactly what I did during those hours in October 1994. I was thinking about how I was going to take a shower in public with only a sarong covering me and with ice-cold water to pour over my dirty body. I was wondering what we were going to be served for dinner. Not frogs again, I hoped. I wasn't looking forward to the visits to the toilet. It really was nothing more than a hole in the ground with four bamboo walls around it. Sharing that hole with fifty others did not make it any better.

Then I moved on to think about things that weren't so self-centered. What made me any different from the people in the truck with me? We wore different clothes and we obviously had dissimilar toothbrushing techniques. But didn't they also have a lot in common with me? What were their dreams and hopes? A safe place to live, a home, family, a safe future for their children, friends they could trust, joy and laughter, the freedom to make decisions about their lives. My dream was that we would be able to afford to buy a car soon. They may have planned to buy a new cow. On the surface we were different, in appearance and dreams, but at the core, were we not quite similar? Then I had to ask myself if what I sought after was more important than what they wanted.

A lot has changed in the years since my husband and I started working with the Karen refugees from Burma. Their situation hasn't changed much. I have changed. The people we have been working with have taught me about life. They have taught me to live. The question I asked myself in the back of the truck then I still ask myself: "What makes me any different from them?" Just as often I also ask myself: "What if it was me?" "What if it was my child?" "What if it was my home, my husband, my country?"

This book is not a book of facts and statistics. Numbers seldom move my heart. People's stories do. I have written thoughts I have had about life as a refugee. I have tried to imagine myself in their situation. I have compared their lives to mine. I have written stories about people I have met whose stories have moved me. The hope I have is that by reading the reflections, you will feel closer to the refugees from Burma.

I hope you will start to think about the 1.5 million people who are on the run from a brutal military dictatorship as individuals with feelings, dreams, fears and hopes just like yourself. Each one of them is a person who was created in God's image. Each one of them has the right to be heard and the right to live. I want to help make that happen. You can also help make it happen. Learning to care is the first step.

NUMBERS SELDOM MOVE MY HEART. PEOPLE'S STORIES DO.

"WITH THEIR INFANTS TIED CLOSE TO THEM
THEY PERFORMED THE DAY'S TASKS
WITH GRACE AND BEAUTY."

KAREN VILLAGE

The first time I went to a Karen village it rained and was dark. There were no streetlights to guide us through the jungle. Instead we had to trust the light of the moon and the sure steps of our Karen friends. They hardly found it challenging to follow the trail that would lead us to the remote hill tribe village right on the Thai-Burma border.

One of our Karen guides carried a toilet on his head. It would be the first toilet in the village. I got the task of carrying all the drinking water. We were on a mission!

The sound of rice being pounded in a big mortar mixed with the multi-pitched cock-a-doodle-doos of the village's many roosters woke me up the next morning. The mountains and hills surrounding the village felt like a fortress that would protect us from any harm. The laughter of children running around in the village was contagious and refreshing. As rocks were used for games and bugs provided great entertainment for little people, I wondered: Who needs Toys R Us?

In the bamboo houses built on stilts sat women on the floor weaving their cloths in colors so bright and happy I knew they had gotten the inspiration from the wild flowers in the jungle. With their infants tied close to them they performed the day's tasks with grace and beauty. Their innocence was revealed in the joy they showed at simple pleasures, such as a balloon thrown in the air, a baby walking clumsily or a huge white person with a camera stuck on his face. With a pipe in the corner of their mouths and big smiles that exposed black teeth it was easy to see the amusement such things provided.

The men gave new meaning to the word masculine. Their muscles were well proportioned and defined. It was the result, not of weightlifting at a gym, but of hard work on the fields and in the jungle. With bows and arrows on their shoulders they purposefully headed for the jungle where they would hunt for wildlife. Their high cheekbones and rugged tanned faces let me know that these were men who had been in battles before, be it with a tiger or a soldier from the enemy's side.

I sat down to eat breakfast that consisted of freshly harvested rice, eggs that were laid that morning and vegetables and herbs that had been picked by the edge of the jungle. After the meal I would shower under the ice cold water that came from a stream in the mountains.

The world of microchips and MP3s, of fast cars and 747s, of microwave popcorn and drive-through fast food, belonged to a different planet.

TRUE RICHES

In the West we spend a lot of time trying to avoid feeling alive. Let me explain:

We cry if our hamburgers don't come with the right topping and our coffee isn't served at the ideal temperature and with the perfect amount of caffeine. We spend fortunes on beds that help us sleep without feeling that we do. We spray everything with cleansers to sterilize our environment from dirt and germs. We buy things in bulk so that we don't ever need to worry about running out of anything. And yet we can go shopping 24 hours a day at stores that rarely are more than a mile away.

We can get pills for everything so we never have to feel pain. We do not need to have a stuffy nose. We can lose weight without feeling hungry. We can exercise without having to go outside, feeling hot or cold. We can watch TV when we drive. We don't want to wait for more than three minutes for our lunch. We can return anything we do not like: our dinner, expired Pop-Tarts or a shirt with a stripe in the wrong color.

Our houses are designed to provide the ultimate comfort. There are many bathrooms. The carpets are soft. The dishwasher must never be broken. We make clothes with no seams so we do not have to feel them. We own different pairs of shoes for every activity we engage in so that our feet will not hurt and our performance will be maximized. We make sure we do not work too many hours in a week so we don't get too tired. We struggle to find things we want for Christmas. Our children are bored with their toys. We have storage rooms for the stuff that we don't need right now. We want to buy new cars once every few years. We have preferences and stick to them: We prefer Coke rather than Pepsi, Ranch rather than Italian dressing, white rather than dark meat on the turkey, Lucky Charms rather than Grape-Nuts. We do not like to be told that our preference is not available.

Our goal in life is that we should not want for anything, nor should we feel any unpleasant emotions such as pain or boredom.

I started thinking about all this while spending time in a refugee camp a while ago. A refugee often does not even own one pair of shoes. A refugee sleeps on a bamboo floor. A mat sometimes serves as a mattress. A refugee eats whatever is available in the camp. Sometimes that is only rice and a clear broth with some onions in it. A refugee is lucky if he owns two shirts. A refugee does not choose where to live, what to eat, what to wear, how many rooms she would like in her house.

How different our lives are from the lives of these refugees. And yet, as I watch the refugees commune together over their simple meals, I question if we are truly richer than they are.

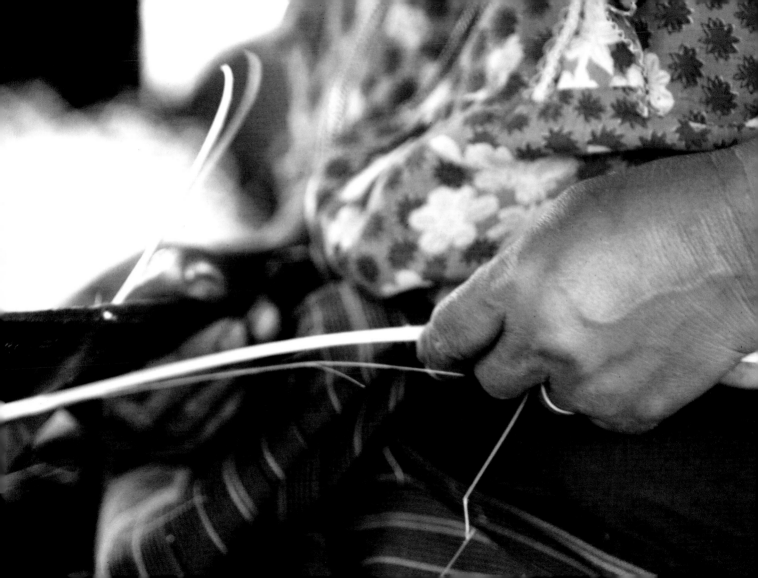

"THE WORLD WANTS US TO THINK

THAT IT IS THE BEST LOOKING,

THE SMARTEST AND THE STRONGEST WHO REALLY MATTER.

THE STRAIGHT A PEOPLE."

ELECTROPLATING AND BUTTERFLIES

There has been a depressing development in my life. When I was nineteen I thought I knew most things about everything; now I am finding out that I know less and less. For example, only recently did I find out that butterflies never eat anything, and I had no idea what electroplating was. I think I know now, but I am not sure I can explain it very intelligently.

At nineteen I also felt that the world's most challenging tasks would not be too difficult for me. Reaching the Himalayas' peaks sounded like a walk in the park. Now I find it hard to conquer the mountains of dirty dishes.

There are times that I ask myself what I can contribute in this world where somebody could do a better job than me at pretty much everything, except maybe using my silly voice while reading about Kristin's favorite mouse at night before she goes to bed.

My neighbor and good friend probably didn't know how much she encouraged me one day while I shared with her my doubts about my abilities to do something. "I could never do that!" I said with more conviction than a used car salesman. "You could too," my neighbor responded, so convincing that I believed her. We talked some more and I went home feeling a little bit better about myself.

Later that day I heard new stories of terror and abuse against the ethnic minorities in Burma. Along with the feelings of anger and despair, came thoughts that reminded me of my limitations. Did I actually think that I could make a difference in the world, in Burma, or in my own neighborhood for that matter? Did I not have a lot in common with the little mouse I read about at night to my 4-year-old? A mouse trying to fight an elephant, is it? "I don't think I could do it," said the familiar voice in my head as I thought of trying to help, trying to bring change in one of the world's worst dictatorships. And I remembered my neighbor's comeback from earlier that day: "You could too!"

I think that I commit a sin when I look at myself and count my shortcomings, my lack of skills and talents. It's OK to be realistic, and say that I probably cannot play the cello for the school concert, especially since I have never actually held one. But it is another thing to compare myself to the great cello players of the world, and conclude that my value as a human being is in question because I am not as good as they are.

The world wants us to think that it is the best looking, the smartest and the strongest who really matter. The straight A people. Only a few fit into that category, and I am certainly not one of them. But look closely: It's not always the straight A people who bring about the biggest changes. It seems to me that it is the ones who are humble enough to admit their limitations, but who nevertheless listen to a neighbor who says: "You can do it!"

I have been reading about the heroes of the world with my children. Among them I have found dyslexic people, prime ministers who have had to repeat a year of elementary school, people with poor health, many with so little money that they had to pray for bread to feed their children. Not often did people change their world thanks to their good looks. Brad Pitt may be able to—who knows? The biggest heroes are the ones who have been faithful to what they have been given and who have listened when God has called them. I want to be one of those people. Mother Teresa once said: "God did not call me to be successful. He called me to be faithful." Comforting, but at the same time challenging.

Can I explain to you how it is that the words I write on my computer fly out of my house and land in my friends' computers across the world when I hit Send? Not a chance. How likely is it that I will ever ascend one of the peaks of the Himalayas? About as likely as it is that my kids will never again have to be told to pick up after themselves.

But can I hug an orphan? Can I tell whoever comes across my path about a war that has lasted more than 50 years in Burma? Can I give of my time and resources to the people who have been robbed of their livelihood and who have suffered more than human beings should ever have to? Can I use the gifts God has given me to help others rather than promoting myself? Yes, I can, and yes, I can.

And besides, there are books that explain how computers work, I can take cello lessons if I want to and I can take a walk up the tallest mountain in Chiang Mai. There's a paved road all the way to the top!

Photo by Stu Corlett

THANKSGIVING

We are in a refugee camp housing thousands of people who have fled a war. Bugs are buzzing around our sweaty bodies. There is no breeze to move the hot air. Little children are playing. From a house close by we hear music. Several people must be gathered together. They are singing in beautiful harmony. Praise songs. "Is there a church meeting?" I ask. "No, one family is having a Thanksgiving service," my friend replies. "Thanksgiving for what?" "For all the good things God has given us over the past few months and for his faithfulness. Most Christian families have a Thanksgiving service twice a year to remember what God has done for them."

How many times a year do I conduct a Thanksgiving service to remember what I have received? These people who are singing praises to God right now are refugees who have lost everything they own. They do not even have a birth certificate. They are some of the poorest people in the world. But they are thankful. They are thankful that they are still alive, that they have food to eat and a floor to sleep on. They are so much bigger than me.

"WHILE WALKING I WAS THINKING OF HOW MANY
UNIQUE KAREN PEOPLE I HAD MET OVER THE YEARS.
SO MANY STORIES, SO MANY DIFFERENT CHARACTERS.
THEY WERE NOT JUST REFUGEES WITHOUT PERSONALITY;
THEY ALL HAD THEIR INDIVIDUAL STORIES
THAT SHOULD BE TOLD AND REMEMBERED."

MEETING POO-POO AND PEE-PEE

"Hi, won't you come and visit Poo-poo and Pee-pee?" a voice asked in perfect English. Walking down the steep hill in Um Pien refugee camp, we turned around and saw a good-looking Karen man dressed in Western clothes. We thought it was a good idea, so we turned around and followed the English-speaking fellow.

He took us to a small bamboo hut, not much different than any of the other huts in the camp. We took off our shoes and climbed up the ladder to the crowded living room, which also served as a sleeping room and kitchen.

On the floor, legs crossed and with long gray hair and beard, sat an old man. On his head, hiding most of his mane was a big knitted hat. He was dressed in the traditional Karen sarong, which is like a skirt that you wrap around your waist. "Hello," he said, "I am Poo-poo. I am a British soldier." At first I thought the man was crazy, but then I remembered that Poo-poo in Karen means Grandfather. And when I looked at the man in front of me, it dawned on me that he was old enough to have fought with the British during World War II. He started telling us part of his story, which no doubt had enough events in it to fill a book, when his wife came in.

A few years younger than her husband, she was no less cute. She smiled at us and introduced herself as Pee-pee, which is Karen for Grandma. She ducked under a curtain that separated one part of their room from the other, and came out with a bag of stale crackers that she served us. To me it seemed quite possible those crackers were from WWII also.

"Now," said Poo-poo, wanting to take charge of the situation, "I want to introduce you to my sons." We of course wanted to meet the offspring from such an interesting couple. "My first son," Poo-poo said with a lot of pride, "is Billy Graham." "He is a pastor," his wife added, equally proud. From under the curtain Billy Graham came out and shook our hands. He told us how he had studied at Bible school and now pastored a church in the refugee camp.

"My next son," Poo-poo continued, not wanting to lose our attention, "is Billy Sunday." "He is the musician," Pee-pee added, obviously proud of him too. Billy Sunday came out, and was definitely just as impressive as his brother Billy Graham. Billy Sunday was the worship leader in Billy Graham's church.

"Now you will meet my third son," said Poo-poo. "His name is Marvelous Jerry, but we call him just Marvelous." Marvelous Jerry must have been waiting behind the curtain, because as soon as his father said his name he was in the room. We never did settle what position Marvelous had in the church, but we were sure it must have been an important one.

"My fourth son," Poo-poo said, "is not with us today." Then I could have sworn he said his fourth son's name was Guacamole. "He is our youngest," Pee-pee let us know.

After introducing us to most of the family, Poo-poo announced that now we should take a picture of them. Pee-pee ran behind the curtain again and came out with a proper hat and a suit jacket that was several sizes too big for Poo-poo. "Now, Poo-poo, you must put this on," she commanded. This was done in a voice that nobody dared argue with. The knitted hat came off and was replaced with the good Sunday hat. To complete the outfit she helped Poo-poo put on the jacket which must have belonged to a giant.

Billy Sunday's stained shirt was covered with a relatively clean white T-shirt. The other two sons did not get to change. Perhaps they did not have any more clean shirts or perhaps Pee-pee thought they looked fine. She herself took a quick look in the small broken mirror that hung on the wall next to a faded photo of the king and queen of Thailand. She seemed to like what she saw. At least she did not try to improve her image. They were ready for the photo session.

We took lots of pictures of them. In true Karen fashion they never cracked a smile. Pictures are serious business. When we were done, they smiled and thanked us, and let us know it was time for us to leave. We said good-bye and continued on our walk down to the car.

While walking I was thinking of how many unique Karen people I had met over the years. So many stories, so many different characters. They were not just refugees without personality; they all had their individual stories that should be told and remembered. I promised myself that next time I went to Um Pien refugee camp, I would stop by Poo-poo and Pee-pee's house and hear the rest of their story.

WHY DO I LET THESE THINGS GET TO ME MORE THAN THE STORIES OF THE PEOPLE THAT WE ARE WORKING WITH? WHY DOESN'T THEIR INTOLERABLE SUFFERING AFFECT ME THE WAY A BAD TRAFFIC JAM IN CHIANG MAI DOES?

THE SMALL STUFF

The small stuff tends to run my life. The clutter. The dishes. The phone calls I haven't made. A perfectly good day can turn into a nightmare for me just because the things I had planned can't happen.

It is the muddy shoes, the misplaced books, the neighbor's rooster. It is realizing that yet another day will pass during which I have not been able to cross off all the things on my to-do list. Why do I let these things get to me more than the stories of the people that we are working with? Why doesn't their intolerable suffering affect me the way a bad traffic jam in Chiang Mai does?

I am often embarrassed by my own small world. You might think that being an aid worker takes away one's selfish heart and replaces it with one purely motivated by love and concern for the poor and needy. Don't be fooled! I am reminded again and again of my own need to seek God's heart. I need His grace to be able to feel the pain that the refugees feel. I need to hear their stories and look at their faces with Jesus in mind. It is only with God's help that I will be able to put aside my own desires and self-centered worries.

Does the small stuff matter that much? There are people in Burma who are dying for their faith right now. There are young men and women who are watching their children die from lack of food or medicine. There are people who are carrying ammunition twice their body weight because they know torture and death await them if they protest. There are children who are crying for their mummies and daddies in the dark night.

In light of that, the mess on the kitchen counter becomes a small burden. In light of that I feel challenged to spend my days doing better things with the gifts God has given me than worrying about my need for more RAM on my computer or when to get the car cleaned.

The grocery shopping still has to be done. The garbage can will always be full. My hope is that I will start feeling closer to the refugees on a daily basis to help me remember that life is about more than the small stuff.

SHOOTING AT KIDS

While I took my girls horseback riding on the 27th of March 2006, Little Naw Eh Ywa Paw was running for her life. She was 9 years old. In front of her was her dad. He was strong and fast. It appeared he was the leader of the group. He carried his old mother on his back. Behind Naw Eh Ywa Paw were her mother, her little sister and her baby brother, as well as the rest of the villagers who were escaping with them. They were running from soldiers with guns. Soldiers that wanted to kill them to remove them from their land. Up on a hill Naw Eh Ywa Paw, her dad and grandmother met the soldiers and the barrels of their guns. Bang.

Her dad and grandmother were killed at close range. Naw Eh Ywa Paw was shot in her stomach, but kept on running until she got help. The rest of the villagers were able to escape. They met a relief team that was able to take the bullet from Naw Eh Ywa Paw's stomach and treat her so that she was able to recover.

They are still hiding in the jungle. There is no dad to watch over them and help provide for them. There is no grandma to help look after the children and tell goodnight stories from when she was a little girl. There is only the hope that they may be able to return to their homes one day. But then, what kind of hope is that? How are they going to survive? Who will help them run their small farm? What will happen when the soldiers decide to attack them again?

I have thought a lot of Naw Eh Ywa Paw. I saw the photos of her and talked to the people who helped treat her. Her story made me angry and hopeless. It made me angry that innocent people could be shot at close range by soldiers whose souls are so corrupted that shooting a 9-year-old little girl with the intent of killing her seems like mere routine. How sick is it that an honest man carrying his ailing mother will lose his life because he is considered an inconvenience? What value do lives have in a nation where you are allowed to kill old toothless ladies with no questions asked afterwards?

It made me hopeless, because this incident is not the only one of its kind. It happens all the time. I wonder why it keeps happening and the stories are never told. We read the news and who Jessica Simpson dates is more important that two lines about the tyranny in Burma. The price of gas is a more important topic of conversation than talking about the fact that in Burma they bury children alive.

Burma is a sick nation, but it makes me wonder if our values are too. I wonder what could be different in Burma today if more people cared. Could Naw Eh Ywa Paw's father and grandmother have been saved? Would the people in her village be living peacefully in their homes instead of hiding somewhere in the jungle without food or shelter? It is impossible to tell.

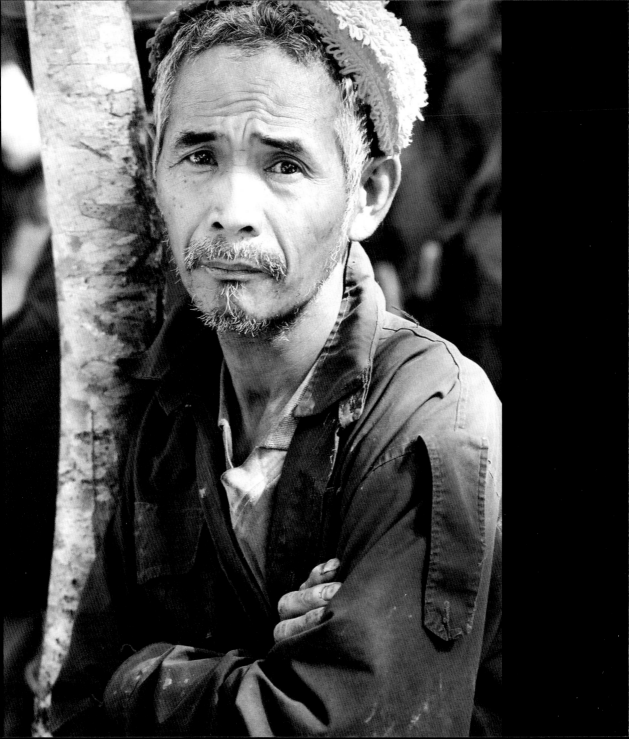

BRAVE

A number of people make the mistake of thinking that just because I live and do what I do, I am brave. To that I can only quote Alanis Morissette, who at times is rather shocking in her honest statements: "I am brave, but I am chicken sh_t." In my own words that means that I am almost always only brave when I know that I will be OK in the end.

There are many who are not like me in this. They are the people who throw themselves from cliffs to see if they can fly, who risk their lives climbing the highest mountains in the world, crossing the North Pole on skis or chasing snakes for fun. It is impressive to see some of these folks defy natural laws such as gravity. But to be honest, most of the time I wonder: Why?

Occasionally I pretend I am a journalist interviewing myself. This could be a sign of insanity, but I hope not. The good thing about these interviews is that I get to decide the questions and the answers. This is what I would say if I asked myself who I thought was brave in this world:

It is the men and women who risk their lives by going to the jungles of Burma to help the displaced people there. I have met them and heard their stories and no extreme-sport-adrenaline-addicted-adventure-seeker can match the courage of these people. With their back-packs holding all their earthly possessions they trek into the jungle, fully aware that they are walking into the territory of the enemy, and if they are caught it will mean a painful and certain death. They walk for days and often for nights through the unfriendly and dangerous terrain of the rainforest, climbing mountains and crossing rivers.

They get sick with malaria or other tropical diseases; they are chased and shot at by the enemy; there are days that they hardly have any food to eat. Some of them die. Do you remember Alias on TV? It is not like that in real life. Sidney would always pull off one of her karate moves in the end and escape relatively unscratched. These people have experienced that the karate moves do not always save you and that you cannot win all the time.

By now I have finished the page in my journalist notebook. I finish a sentence with unreadable scribble and look up and ask: Why are these people doing this? What is it that drives them?

The answer is already on the tip of my tongue: They do it to save people's lives. They do it out of love. You want to know what brave is. That is brave.

AMAZING HARMONIES

The thing I remember the most from my first few visits to a Karen refugee camp is not the sad stories they told me nor the smell of thousands living crammed together in a confined area. It is the music.

There is always music. Not from the radio or a CD player, but from people singing and playing the guitar. Songs are sung by people not only with their voices, but with their hearts as well. Music is played by masters who can make the cheapest Burmese guitar sound like Pat Metheny has just come to town. Songs are sung in amazing harmonies at every church gathering. Music is heard in front of people's houses at any time of the day. They will use their idle hours waiting for refugee life to end to sing songs of praise and worship to a God that they know has not left them. It's music that expresses a depth of faith and trust that I can only hope I would have if ever I had to walk in their shoes.

PRAYING

Since I am a Christian, and one who takes my faith seriously, it is only natural that I pray for the refugees regularly. I pray that they will be safe. I pray that they will have food to eat. I pray that I will be able to help them. I pray that along with many other things.

There isn't anything wrong with my prayers, except that I often do not have much of my heart involved in them. They fit in the same category as my prayers before a meal. It is a routine that I have been fooled into believing that God enjoys hearing.

I am a Christian so I better say a prayer before I eat so God won't get angry and poison the food. I work with refugees, so I need to throw in a prayer for them along with the request for good sleep and nice weather tomorrow.

There is another kind of prayer. It is when I believe that God is actually there with me while I am talking to Him. I can ask for his intervention on behalf of the refugees. In order to do that, I need to imagine myself in their situation.

If I think of myself as the mother whose baby is burning with a fever from suspected malaria, my prayer will not just be a rattling of quick words, but my prayers will be said with urgency and desperation.

If I imagine myself as the young girl who is about to be raped by a group of dark and dirty soldiers, I will not merely look at my watch and decide that it is time to stop the prayer meeting, but I will weep to God in despair and horror.

If I imagine myself as the 13-year-old boy who has been forced to become a soldier and who has been commanded to kill innocent people, I will not use the same words in my prayers that I use to pray for a good night's sleep, but I will plead with the God who is my only hope, the only one who can rescue me and deliver me from this evil.

If I imagine myself as the husband who is led away to be executed together with the other men in his village because they did not comply with the demands of the enemy, I will call out to God for righteousness to prevail and for evil to come to an end.

If I imagine myself as the little child who has seen her parents die and who has nowhere to go, I will pray with the heart of God himself.

THERE IS ANOTHER KIND
OF PRAYER. IT IS WHEN I
BELIEVE THAT GOD IS
ACTUALLY THERE WITH
ME WHILE I AM TALKING
TO HIM.

INTENSE LOVE

Before I had kids I thought I could handle anything. Running 15 km in the tropics? Bring it on! Eating the chicken that just was executed in front of my eyes? Sad, but I can do it. Learning new languages and relating to people who don't at all think like my Western brain does? No problem.

Then I had three kids. I wasn't prepared for what that would do: It brought out the best and the worst in me.

I never knew that I could get so fiercely angry or that I was as selfish as it turned out I was. The extent of my impatience reached far beyond the boundaries of what should be tolerated by humans. On the other hand I never knew that I could love somebody so intensely, so completely and with so much joy either. I know what a mother's heart is like now, not only in theory, but in real life.

This has helped me feel the pain of the refugee mothers in a new way. A couple of years into motherhood it dawned on me that refugee women feel the exact same way about their children as I do. They love their babies. They want the very best future for their sons and daughters. They hurt when their children hurt. They like to talk about their kids' achievements or their naughty behaviors to willing and unwilling listeners. The big difference is that they do not have the opportunities I have.

Being a parent has also let me see children for who they really are: Intriguing, challenging and all-consuming in their need for attention. They are hard to control and seldom fit into molds that we try to squeeze them into. They are as passionate in their love as they are in their hate. Their characters are as different as fish sticks and Tootsie Rolls. They are fun, they are messy, they are unpredictable; they are people with opinions and convictions. That is why I love them so much.

Children who are the victims of war can be all this and much more too. There are boys and girls in the refugee camps that I have visited who can be every bit as mischievous as my own kids. Behind their dirty faces and messy hair are people who can collect bugs in jars, tell stories about heroes and monsters, who can draw pictures of pretty flowers and butterflies as well as rocket-ship-cars. Their legs can take them on adventures to secret hiding places or on a chase after a ball. Their hands can hold little kittens or dolls, with their tiny fingers they will softly stroke it as if it was their own baby.

Life is much different for a child of war, but much is also the same. I feel I have gotten to understand them a little better than I used to. My own children have taught me.

BEING A PARENT
HAS ALSO LET ME
SEE CHILDREN FOR
WHO THEY REALLY
ARE: INTRIGUING,
CHALLENGING AND
ALL-CONSUMING IN
THEIR NEED FOR
ATTENTION.

A TRUCK FULL OF HOPE

Just as I turned off the engine, thinking that I was done driving, my husband called and told me I wasn't. Some small people down the road needed a ride to a Christmas party. It was time to make an illegal U-turn on the highway that serves as the border between the refugee camp and the rest of the world.

I drove the 500 meters back to the next entrance to the camp. I hoped I remembered exactly where it was so I would not have to make one more of those turns!

I should not have worried! Before me, like a field of white lilies, were the children I had been sent to pick up. Their Karen clothes were so white it was a stunning contrast to all the brown around us. They were 4-and 5-year-old miniature people with one goal in mind: To get themselves onto the bed of my truck.

When all 20 of them were safely seated in the back of my muddy truck we ventured down the highway. I was driving the most valuable cargo I had ever transported. Sitting behind me was the future of a nation. Their white clothes became for me the symbol of their innocence and the future I wished to give them. The mud on my unwashed truck was a serious threat to the white outfits they were all wearing, but they skillfully squatted above it. Neither could the threat of a brutal military regime and the unjust lack of educational opportunities ruin the positive attitude of these children. They were giggling and chatting with each other under the blazing sun.

They were going to sing and perform. They were going to receive a Christmas present. I drove a truck full of hope.

THEIR WHITE CLOTHES BECAME FOR ME THE SYMBOL OF THEIR INNOCENCE AND THE FUTURE I WISHED TO GIVE THEM.

MY ANGER-TRIGGERS

"It just comes by itself," my daughter Kristin says when she cries and screams. I have found it is her way of avoiding the real issue: she is out of control.

I tend to let my selfishness spill out and take different forms, depending on the situation, too. I do not throw myself on the floor while screaming and kicking, so you could say my approach is a bit more mature. I usually do not hit people nor do I pull their hair. I try my best to share my stuff. We are in different stages of our lives, Kristin and I; she is 4 and I have seen my first grey hair. But sometimes I wonder if I handle my frustrations any better than my daughter who is just now finding out that the world does not revolve around her.

I do my best cussing while in traffic. You have to understand that to drive in Thailand during any rush hour is a test that most of us fail. We usually end up at the right destination, but not without sinning with our thoughts, words and actions. If the computer has the nerve to hang up on me I hit it repeatedly with my index finger to let it know I am extremely displeased. I say insensitive and mean things to my kids and my husband just because I am tired or frustrated. In my heart I slap people who cut in front of me when I am waiting in line. I have thrown books at people who disagree with me and spread butter in my sister's face once when I was mad.

When I look at the list of anger-triggers, most of them are things that only affect me and my own little world. How about exchanging them for some anger about the injustice on the planet? I would like to become angrier about the villages that have been burned to the ground leaving thousands homeless. I would like to become angrier about the men and women who are slaves for soldiers that abuse them and torture them in any fashion they want. I would like to be angrier when I hear about children who have been thrown into the fire and killed or about little girls that have been used as sex slaves before their first tooth fell out. I would like to feel anger when I hear about little boys used as soldiers, carrying guns that weigh more than they do.

I think that is the kind of anger that pleases God and that sparks action. That is the kind of anger I will not be embarrassed for my children to see in me. That is the kind of anger that can change the lives of people.

WHEN I LOOK AT THE LIST OF ANGER-TRIGGERS, MOST OF THEM ARE THINGS THAT ONLY AFFECT ME AND MY OWN LITTLE WORLD.

DECEMBER

December is the month of the year when I am most stressed.

There is so much giving, so many family traditions that I need to uphold, tons of crafts that I feel we must make, smells that must be smelled, tastes that must be tasted. I have to be kind, and there are those bothersome cards that someone has decided must be sent out before Christmas. Why can't we send them in September?

My muscles get tense thinking of who may be giving us Christmas presents that we have not had the foresight or the finances to give to first. What will they think? I try so hard to enjoy myself and have a great time that I get headaches and PMS daily. Sweet December.

In the hills that belong to the Karen people of Burma, people do not feel the pressure of buying more expensive gifts for their kids than the neighbors did. They seldom have to worry about the extra pounds they will put on due to December gluttony. They may have to endure the predictable sound of Rudolph the Red Nosed Reindeer, but not from the loudspeakers at shopping malls.

Starting December 1st they sit outside under the stars and sing Christmas songs. This they do every night for the whole month. They sing. They make fires to sit around. They practice their harmonies as they fill the dark nights with praises to God, with songs of thanks to Jesus, hymns declaring that He came to give us life, and that He died and rose again. They call it Sweet December. It is so simple, so pure and so right. Somewhere along the way I have lost it among all my activities. The sweetness of December is not in the cookies and homemade candies, but rather in the fellowshipping with brothers and sisters who have experienced the hope that Jesus' birth gave us. It is in looking up at the stars in the dark evening telling Jesus: "I am glad you came."

THEY FILL THE DARK
NIGHTS WITH PRAISES
TO GOD, WITH SONGS OF
THANKS TO JESUS

DECORATION

Flowers in empty tomato paste cans and plastic water bottles. Seven-year-old calendars decorating the walls. Magazine pictures of Paul Newman, Princess Diana and cute white babies. Gold streamers with Happy New Year printed on them. Refugees may be forced to live in substandard conditions, but this does not take away their desire to make their surroundings feel like home. They use whatever they can find to make their temporary homes as pretty and bright as possible.

Whenever I visit their homes I can't help comparing them to my house so full of stuff that I can't find room for it all. The next time I am annoyed that the pillows on my couch do not match the color of the curtains; please remind me of the calendar from 1987 that was good enough to decorate the only room in the house of a refugee family I once went to visit.

HAPPINESS AND SHOPPING

Yesterday I thought that if I could only have a complete new outfit from J. Jill I would surely be happy and not want for anything. Then I put on an old outfit that was *so* the wrong color and style, and I had a pretty good day anyway. Like most of the human race, I have the idea that more and more stuff will make me happier. This isn't always the case, although I must admit that new clothes give me a good feeling.

I would like a nice house with a spectacular view and the latest patio furniture to go with it. When I go to a mall, I hear the stuff calling my name. Seriously. I am materialistic at the core, even though I try my best to disguise it. Interestingly, when I think back on my happiest times over the last years, they are not the times when I got new stuff.

We bought a new car seven years ago. It was the nicest one we had ever had. It had power windows and an automatic lock. And I can honestly tell you that I do not remember the day we got it. That's how important that day was! Now ask me if I remember picking wild raspberries in Norway with my daughters! Oh, yes.

My happiest times always involve the people I love. It can be as simple as a cup of coffee and an uninterrupted talk with my husband or as complex as watching my daughters perform at a ballet recital. It can be sitting together on our couch while watching an exciting movie or going for hikes in the mountains while the wind is blowing. The main thing is that we are doing things as a family. Our scrapbooks and hard drive are full of pictures of the Gumaers doing things together. We are making gingerbread men & women before Christmas, dressing up in weird costumes, riding our bikes in pouring rain or eating sticky rice and chicken by a Thai waterfall. These are memories that I treasure more than any possession I own. They are times when I have experienced the intense feeling of love and happiness. Among our family photos I cannot find one picture of us shopping.

I occasionally get the feeling that the refugees we interact with consider us supremely happy. If our possessions are the measure of our happiness then we certainly rank high on the list of contented people. I would like them to understand that while it is true that I am happy, it is not necessarily because of all the gadgets I own. My happiness comes from being loved and giving love.

But here comes the tricky part: I don't think they will believe me. I think they will look at all my stuff and they will wonder if I would still say I was happy if I lost it all. They may take a look at all my belongings and wonder why I don't give them away if it does not matter to me. It makes me wonder too. Is it true that I would be just as happy without all my stuff, or is it just a cliché that I use because I have never been so poor that I did not own anything?

THESE ARE MEMORIES
THAT I TREASURE MORE
THAN ANY POSSESSION I
OWN. THEY ARE TIMES
WHEN I HAVE
EXPERIENCED THE
INTENSE FEELING OF
LOVE AND HAPPINESS.
AMONG OUR FAMILY
PHOTOS I CANNOT FIND
ONE PICTURE OF US
SHOPPING.

"WHAT DID JESUS WANT US TO DO?
HOW MUCH DID WE HAVE TO LOVE
OUR NEIGHBOR?"

DO UNTO OTHERS

It was getting close to the end of the day and we were eating cod and pink mashed potatoes. There was a good feeling around the big table. We had been playing in the pool and helping each other with the dinner. I thought my husband had finally decided to start having family devotions when he cut through our talk about how to do a perfect crawl stroke: "You know how Jesus told us to do to others as we would like them to do to ourselves. What do you think that means to us?" he said sounding pastoral.

As if they had already rehearsed the answer to this question, the girls answered almost simultaneously: "Well, it means that we should be nice to other people and help them."

Although the answer was right, it wasn't good enough: "Yes, but how much should we help them then? I mean, think about the refugees in the jungle that I just found out about. I feel we are not doing enough for them. What do Jesus' words to us really mean?"

"Daddy, what do you want us to say? I do not know why you are asking us this." The atmosphere around the table was getting a little tense. It was an uncomfortable question. What did Jesus want us to do? How much did we have to love our neighbor? Our neighbors right then were 18,000 displaced people hiding somewhere in Burma's jungles. The monsoon rain had taken them by surprise. They needed plastic sheeting to hide under. They needed food, medicines, clothes and safety. What would we have wanted others to do for us if we had been in their situation?

Elise had tears in her eyes. "Do we need to sell our piano then?" Naomi was getting a bit agitated: "I don't want to sell our house and live in the jungle." Kristin was not sure what was going on. She wanted dessert. I wished that Jesus had not been so straightforward in his teachings. It seemed like he really meant what he had said and I had to do something about it.

In the end we did not sell our house or the piano, and we did have dessert. But we made some changes in our lives. For the following weeks the children gave all their allowance and the extra money they made by doing chores to the IDPs. We worked a little harder, gave a little more and prayed that our efforts would be multiplied.

But I am still asking myself what exactly I should do about Jesus' teachings. I love the verses that say things like: "Do not worry" and "Ask and you shall receive". But if these promises are true, then I must also take seriously the challenge to love my neighbor like myself and to do to others as I would want them do to me. When my neighbors become the poorest people of the world and I belong to the world's richest percentile then it could be that I will be asked to give a bit more than what feels comfortable.

A NEW SCRIPT

Some days ago I talked to 14-year-old Nang Tawng, who, at the age of seven, was tied to a tree by Burmese soldiers. From there she was forced to watch her mother being raped and then shot. She was a Shan girl living in a Shan army camp alongside more than two hundred other orphans who had very similar stories.

Her life was real. She sat right across from me as she was talking. Her eyes were focused on the rocks on the ground as she was trying to keep the facts of her story straight and not feel anything while she was sharing. Her long hair was tied in a ponytail. Her face was plain, but pretty. I can still hear her quiet voice speaking if I close my eyes. "Kruu hon," she replied when I asked her what she wants to become when she grows up. She wants to become a teacher. Most of her people are illiterate. Maybe with knowledge they can conquer the enemy.

I find it hard to care about "stuff" since coming home from the mountains where I met Nang Tawng. It felt a little bit like I was walking into a movie.

The decisions I have to make about dinner and sleepovers seem overwhelming. Something tells me that true life is up there on the mountain I just left.

Nang Tawng told me she had everything she needed there in the army camp. I saw that. She had a mat to sleep on in a room of 25 other girls. She had all her clothes and other belongings in a cardboard box in front of her mat. I gave her a small wallet that had a pink lipstick in it. She said that if we really wanted to give her something, some paper to write on would be nice.

Before I met Nang Tawng I had been a little upset that I cannot buy organic food here and that I did not have any new music for my runs. I was annoyed that my stomach was not flat enough and that my hair was too wavy when the air is humid. Now I am trying to focus on what I have rather than what I don't.

I have decided to do whatever is in my might to help a people whose history is full of pain, betrayal and loss, but also mixed with hope, courage and kindness. I think I want to ask for a new script for my life's movie. I do not want the one where materialism and self-centeredness are the main themes. I will replace it with the one that puts the refugees of Burma as the main actors.

> I FIND IT HARD TO CARE ABOUT "STUFF" SINCE COMING HOME FROM THE MOUNTAINS WHERE I MET NANG TAWNG. IT FELT A LITTLE BIT LIKE I WAS WALKING INTO A MOVIE.

"FROM THE REFUGEES I HAVE LEARNED THAT

IF THEY DO NOT BELIEVE IN GOD,

INDEED THEY HAVE NOTHING.

HE IS THEIR ONLY HOPE.

SELDOM HAVE I HEARD THEM BLAME GOD FOR

THEIR SUFFERING."

GOD AND REFUGEES

During my years of knowing refugees and hearing their stories, I have occasionally thought that the people who have suffered this much should not be expected to believe in God, a loving Creator. They should be given access into heaven without the usual requirement of faith.

This of course says more about what I believe about God than it says about Him and the refugees.

As I let my heart pursue a God so very different from what I thought, I am learning what He desires. As I draw close to Him it is clear that He did not make the war and the suffering I have seen and am appalled by. People did that.

From the refugees I have learned that if they do not believe in God, they do indeed have nothing. He is their only hope. Seldom have I heard them blame God for their suffering. Instead they reach out to Him in their pain, in their losses and in their fear. It is through their faith in Him that they find a comfort that calms, heals, and gives purpose.

I do not really understand how they can do this. But I see that their faith is so genuine, so pure and so simple that I seek to learn from them. I want that kind of faith.

I HEAR STORIES OF
MOTHERS WHO HAVE HAD
TO GIVE BIRTH TO THEIR
BABIES IN THE JUNGLE
WHILE THEY ARE
RUNNING AWAY FROM THE
ENEMY.

GIVING BIRTH

There is no bigger event in a woman's life than to give birth. It is a wonderful and terrifying experience all at once. We plan for it from the day we know we are pregnant. We will always remember the doctor who was there to receive our baby, how long it took to push at the end, and whether or not we had stitches. We also assume that it is just as exciting for the rest of the world to hear all the details of the birth from beginning to end.

I hear stories of mothers who have to give birth to their babies in the jungle while they are running away from the enemy. There is no time to recover after the birth. The baby is wrapped in a cloth and carried while the journey continues through dangerous territory. There are no visitors bringing flowers and special treats to the brave mother and presents wrapped in pastel colors for the baby. There are no neatly decorated baby rooms to welcome the little person who has just been born. No infant stimulation toys in black and white are displayed for the newborn. The baby's biggest challenge will be to stay alive. Her mother's biggest challenge will be to make it happen.

GETTING TO A WEDDING

A wedding Karen style is something to look forward to.

I had my camera ready and thought about what would be best to give to the bride and groom since I had never met them before, nor had I known that I was going to their wedding until last night. I had put on my cleanest T-shirt and my new PRANA pants, a gift from my husband. If only I had been able to see myself in the mirror before we stepped out of our bamboo inn! It wasn't very likely that anybody would mistake me for a model of any kind.

I tucked my toilet paper, water bottle and camera in my naturally dyed Karen shoulder bag and wandered off towards the river where we would catch the next boat. We would float down the river David Livingstone-style and end up in the next refugee camp.

The sun had not yet risen above the green mountains surrounding us. These Karen people sure knew how to get the most out of the day. I was looking forward to the leisurely boat trip. The mountains, the jungle and the wide river provided a view that I felt would inspire me to write.

Our boat arrived about an hour after the time we had been told it would show up. There were no apologies offered for that, just a big smile given by the boat owner whose breakfast appeared to be the beetle nut he was chewing. His boat did something to my idea of leisurely. I suddenly started to question whether wood could actually float!

We got into the wobbly thing and sat down. I started planning how to save my camera from destruction in case we rolled over in the river. I looked at the distance from the boat to shore and convinced myself that I could swim that far.

We were off. The boat engine pushed us forward at a speed that felt just right for me. Maybe this was going to work out. I had not finished that thought before the first rapids met us head-on. Oh, it was still the rainy season and the river had a bit more water in it than normal, we were told. Not to worry. This boat had seen worse. That gave me confidence. The boat owner was spitting beetle nut juice while he bravely maneuvered us through the rapids. I could breathe again. My camera would be OK!

Minutes later we were surprised by more rapids. This time we were showered from head to toe with the brown muddy water the river was full of. My idea of becoming a new trendsetter in the Karen refugee camp vanished with the water that rushed over me. Now I was looking at the prospect of becoming the first white person to arrive at a wedding soaking wet.

I should not have worried so much. We made it to the wedding—just as the guests were leaving. They smiled at us as we stood there with our cameras, wet hair and mud stripes down our faces. "These white people have strange customs," they may have thought. Or maybe they were just thinking: "Why do they look so embarrassed? A little water from the river is surely nothing to complain about."

PIPE CLEANERS AND YARN

Pipe cleaners, yarn, modeling clay and other craft supplies are on the bamboo floor of a shack in the camp. It is hot. The only light is the daylight that makes its way through the openings of the rattan walls of the house.

Sitting with us on the floor are about 20 Karen youth. Hardly a word is being said at first. They are all concentrating on their projects. Some are making bookmarks or pictures using different colored yarn. A few are twisting the pipe cleaners into bracelets and other accessories. Others are making smaller creations with the clay. The boys are as eager as the girls to do some cross-stitching.

When some of them are done with what they are making, a big smile and a look of utter satisfaction spreads across their faces. "Look what I made." "I made this. Do you like it?" "Can I actually keep it?" Like little children after drawing their first flower or house, their pride cannot be hidden.

"We have never gotten to do anything like this before," explains one of the older artists. A crayon is a luxury and paper is often just a dream. Latent artistic talent abounds among the refugees. Some of it comes to life in this bamboo shack for an afternoon. We sit with refugees of war who for a while are not in a war, but in a world of color, shapes and artistic forms.

BEAUTY

I think they are beautiful. I don't think I've ever thought the refugees weren't. Not the beauty of perfect bodies and a face free from wrinkles. Not the beauty of brand name clothes. Not the beauty of spotless complexions, perfectly styled hair or smiles of bright white teeth.

They are beautiful because they have lived. In their faces history is written. Their hands tell stories. Their feet are wrinkled and brown from years of walking without good shoes, through jungles and over fields, maybe down the busy streets to the market. Maybe they were running from soldiers as their villages burned in the background. Their clothes were once bright in their colors. Some of them were woven on old looms in their bamboo houses. To add to the already intricate patterns, they added seeds they found in the jungle or in the fields. Now the clothes are faded in their colors. Many of the pretty seeds have fallen out. There are holes in several places.

Still I find their clothes more beautiful than expensive designer outfits from exclusive boutiques. Their backs are straight and their heads lifted high. Often they carry their loads on their heads. The humiliations they have suffered have not made them change their proud stature.

They are beautiful. Their beauty tells a story.

JUNGLE LESSONS

The jungle is so inviting from a distance. Green, lush and mystical with all its sounds and unexpected shapes. Once you are in it, though, it becomes a little intimidating. The sounds are no longer so appealing—they are mystical in an unsettling way; perhaps they are the sounds of snakes, spiders and man-eating plants.

We were hiking through the jungle at night. The beauty could not be seen, but the sounds seemed to grow louder with every step. The flash light did not provide the amount of light necessary to convince me that a boa constrictor was not there hiding somewhere ready to eat me. I tried to act brave.

We came to the hill that was going to be our campsite for the night. Tall trees would provide support for our hammocks. Their leaves would be a welcome shelter from the drizzling rain. I tried to pretend I knew how to hang a hammock. I fooled no one.

My Karen friends led me safely through the jungle through the night. They helped me to carry my heavy backpack. They showed me how to hang my hammock, and then hung it for me when my attempts proved useless. They cut down bamboo in the morning and made a fire so we could get warm. Then they made bamboo cups for us so we could drink tea. They did this with such grace and skill that it made me look like I was a cow trying to gallop like a horse.

It made me grateful for these incredibly gifted and beautiful people I have been given as friends. It made me respect and admire them for their skills, strength and courage. It made me think of myself as their student who has a lot to learn and a lot to gain from knowing them.

"THE JUNGLE IS SO INVITING FROM A DISTANCE.

GREEN, LUSH AND MYSTICAL

WITH ALL ITS SOUNDS AND UNEXPECTED SHAPES."

Photo by Steve Gumaer

THINGS THAT DON'T GO AWAY

There are lots of unpleasant things in my life. Bills are one of them. They come in the mail in their cigarette smoke colored envelopes with a minimalist blank window in front. I open them, read them and put them on the kitchen counter. Sometimes they stay there for a long time. I trick myself into thinking that if I just don't think about them, they will disappear. It hasn't happened yet!

There are talks I do not want to do. People who I wish would be other places than in my life. Issues I wish others would address instead of me. I avoid confrontations like it is a plague. Hoping the conflict will go away if I don't think of it.

Perhaps the mess in the bedroom will go away if I do not go in there. Could it be that by not thinking about them, the calories in the cake I just ate will disappear?

Sometimes I do the same thing with suffering in the world. I turn the switch off in my head and believe that as long as the volume is on mute, there is nothing happening that I need to worry about. As long as I switch the channel on the TV away from upsetting news about children starving to a channel with a relaxing comedy, I am safe. I can't be blamed for something I do not know about.

If I go about my very important business of doing the things that I think are very important, I do not have to think about the uncomfortable stories of children being taken away from their parents and tortured to death, of families hiding in unsafe places with nothing to eat and only each others' horror-stricken faces as a shield of protection against a brutal enemy. If I just do not think about it, it may not actually be happening.

As I continue to grow up I realize that just as the unpaid bills on the kitchen counter do not disappear by ignoring their presence, neither do stories of people suffering unimaginable injustices in the world. I can think about them or I can choose not to. The bills still have to get paid. The poor still need help. The bedroom must still be cleaned. The hungry still need food. The calories in the cake must still be worked off. The cold children in the mountains still need blankets.

I think I am going to go through the pile on the counter and deal with it. After that I need to go through the pile in my head and deal with that. Somewhere in the pile is the challenge to get involved and not just live as if life is a pleasant novel that some romantic lady with fluffy hair and pink nails wrote.

THERE ARE LOTS OF UNPLEASANT THINGS IN MY LIFE. BILLS ARE ONE OF THEM.

TO LOVE A COUNTRY

An interesting thing about people is that we all think that we come from the best country in the world. I do. I come from the country famous for its fjords, mountains and the midnight sun. The people of my country have made important contributions to the world in the areas of peace making, human rights, arts, music, athletics, politics and science. "I am from Norway", I say with pride.

In Thailand I have sat in taxis making small talk with the drivers. "I understand why you are here," they will say. "Isn't Thailand the best country you have ever been to?" Is there an American in the world who doesn't think they come from God's favorite nation? It's the same with the Brazilians and the Swedes, the Indians and the Tongans.

The peoples of Burma are proud of the places they come from too, Karen-state, Shan-state, Kachin-state and many more. They will tell us of their traditions and of the beauty of their land. They are always eager to explain the origin of their special dishes, the games they play and the songs they sing. Their costumes are a source of great pride. There are history and traditions woven into their beautiful clothes.

As they are fighting for their right to exist, we miss out on some of the great contributions they could have given. All their energy and resources are spent on the task of survival for themselves and their people. They don't win gold medals in the Olympics. Their authors do not write books that become best sellers. Their music isn't heard on hit lists everywhere. Their artists have not had their art exhibited in museums around the world. Their scientists do not make breakthroughs in any fields.

I still think that the Karen and the other ethnic groups of Burma have a greater reason to be proud of their states than we do. So what if our countries win gold medals and soccer championships? Just take a look at how these athletes are pampered! Some earn more money than presidents, scientists develop their diets and they spend their entire lives training to become the best. In Norway we have a whole generation of engineers and professors. But isn't that the least we can do considering how spoiled and rich we are!

I wonder what would happen if we put some of the superstar athletes in the jungle for a while where they would have to kill their own food and gather their own fire wood. How would world class musicians like to make their songs on a four-string guitar that they had to share with ten others?

It's easy to become the best when things are handed to us on a silver spoon and there is peace and quiet all around. For the peoples of Burma, nothing comes for free—not even the right to be alive. When they still make music, paint pictures, become doctors and play in soccer tournaments they have every right to smile and say with pride: "I come from Burma."

GOOD KIDS

My kids. I want them to be a little bit better than everybody else's. Not a lot. Just barely. My baby ought to start walking a few weeks earlier than the rest. My second grader ought to read her first chapter book faster than her friends. How about a main part in a school play with all the parents watching? That would be my kindergartener.

I don't only want them to excel academically, in athletics and arts. I want them to have a better character as well. I want them to give their toys away to the refugees without me suggesting it. I want them to gladly give up the comforts of their own warm bed and clean bathroom to go on a trip to the border to play with the orphaned children.

It is not always that easy. My children, like most children, refuse to conform to my idea of a perfect child. They have not read the books I have read and do not understand how adults think about children. When planning for our trip to give the orphans their Christmas gifts early in December, my second grader (who still has not made it through one chapter book) responded like this: "No fair! Why do they get to open their presents before us?" When demanding that they choose some of their toys to give to the refugees, my kindergartener (who is afraid of getting water in her ears and sucks her fingers when she is tired) picked out two broken toys that she did not want any more anyway. When being offered two open arms by a nice Karen lady at the orphanage, my two-year-old (who did not walk until she was 14 months and who has severe temper tantrums in front of people who teach parenting seminars) frowned like she had seen a monster, screamed and turned away.

They do not always perform like we want them to. They are people. They make their own choices. We can only do our best, set a good example and pray.

The 'setting a good example' part gets stuck in my throat lie a glob of peanut butter. What do I sacrifice to help people in need? It is easy to ask my girls to give up a Barbie doll or two. But what do I give up? Don't my offerings sometimes look like broken toys that I do not really need any more?

Is it my character that needs to be worked on? Is it my heart that needs prayer? I hope my children don't spend time comparing me to other moms and wishing that I could be better than average in character, beauty and knowledge. I would fall short.

What I want them to see is a mom who cares about people in need. Somebody who wants to make a difference in the world. Somebody who is as far from perfect as Norway is from Thailand. Somebody who will fall while learning to walk, but who will then get up and try again.

TRUSTING GOD

Some times I feel like a phony. I talk about God as if He is a fancy gadget that can do incredible things for me. Like a toy that needs batteries to do what it has been designed to do. With the right kind of batteries God will work and do miraculous things for me. Trusting God is often meaningless talk that I do to impress people. What do I really trust God with? My life? My future? My children's future? Can I honestly say I trust God with things that really matter? I often don't. When things get a little shaky I come up with my own exit plans, just in case God doesn't do what He is supposed to. Maybe His batteries are a little low. It is good to know that there is Tylenol in case God does not take my headache away. That kind of trusting.

I guess it would be a little different if I had nowhere else to go than to Him. If my husband was sick with a raging fever and there were no doctors, and no medicine other than roots that could be found on the jungle floor. Then I would have to trust God. If the rain was pouring down all night and I knew the hill my small house was sitting on was a mudslide waiting to happen, and there was nothing I could do but to wait it out, then I would have to trust God. If my child was shivering in the cold wearing only the t-shirt she wore when we ran from the village. If she was begging me for something to eat, but the last of the rice had been eaten two days ago, then I would have to trust in God. If I knew that the enemy was somewhere very close by and that if they found our hiding spot in this clearing, we would all die, then I would have to trust God.

My circumstances are never as extreme as those of the refugees who are on the run from the enemy. When I talk about trusting God as a way to get what I want from Him, it is good to remind myself of my brothers and sisters who have to trust Him with their lives on a regular basis. To them God is their source of hope and comfort, He is not a vending machine that drops the right flavored circumstance when correct words and actions are being used. He is instead the battery charger.

WHAT DO I REALLY TRUST GOD WITH? MY LIFE? MY FUTURE? MY CHILDREN'S FUTURE?

TOYLESS PRE-SCHOOL

On the floor in front of me were 70 children. If 'cute' had needed a personification, it could have been found here. The children in the pre-school I was visiting were from 2-5 years old. They were looking at me with a mixture of horror and fascination. Nobody said a word. It could have been because the team and I looked so weird, but I suspected that they were usually quiet.

The walls were missing the colorful posters and pieces of pre-school art that normally decorates any institution that has children in it. In fact, there was not a speck of color on any of the walls.

"What do the children play with when they come here?" I asked one of the caretakers. Her answer surprised me: "We do not have any toys to play with." A pre-school without a single toy! They did not even have a ball. There were no plastic boxes with crayons; there were no shelves with books, no dolls, no blocks, and no posters on the walls with the numbers, the shapes, and the letters of the alphabet.

What surprised me even more was the caretaker's answer when I asked her what they needed the most for the school. She did not ask for toys. She asked for blankets. "It gets so cold here and the children freeze at night," she explained. The toys and the pictures on the walls would have to come second.

The children got up and walked over to the low tables where they were given their lunch. For most of them it was the only meal they would get that day.

"ISN'T IT INTERESTING?" SAID ELISE.

"THEY DO NOT HAVE ANY TOYS TO PLAY WITH

AND STILL THEY ARE PLAYING ALL DAY LONG.

IN SOME WAYS THEY SEEM HAPPIER THAN ALL MY FRIENDS

WHO HAVE SO MUCH."

SHAN TRIP

My daughter and I were on a unique adventure few foreign children aged 10 get to experience. From the back of the Honda Dream Elise and I saw rugged mountains, green fields and dense jungles so fresh and magnificent it made us wonder if it had looked this way since the morning it was created. Up, up, up went the road. Three hours later we were on the top of the world.

We were to spend several days here with a people who know beauty, but also great sorrow and violence. The Shan people are considered a nuisance by the Burmese military junta. Therefore they burn their villages, rape the women, torture and kill anybody whose presence is not desired.

But from the mountaintop where we were, things seemed like perfection. The mountains surrounding us looked like the smaller siblings of the one we were on. The mist covered them like a blanket that the moths had eaten holes in. The women were spots of color and elegance as they moved around the camp, some of them carrying baskets and buckets on their heads. The men added strength to the beauty.

We were sitting on a hill overlooking the life that was happening below us. The children reminded me of playful kittens running to and fro in a never-ending chase of a toy that kept moving.

"Isn't it interesting?" said Elise. "They do not have any toys to play with and still they are playing all day long. In some ways they seem happier than all my friends who have so much." I looked and smiled at my wise daughter. I was proud of the discovery she had made.

Later in the week, after she had found a two-inch long spider by her pillow and had heard endless speeches about the political situation in Burma, Elise had a ball in her hand and about 50 Shan children to play with. She could not speak their language but the ball was what could bring the two cultures together. For four hours they played and laughed. When the sun went down Elise walked back to our bungalow a richer person. She had gained new friendships and memories. The fact that her new friends spoke a different language and had a culture and history very different from her own did not matter.

I learned an important lesson that day: Diplomacy sometimes takes the shape of a ball and a friendly ten-year-old. It was a lesson that I wish many influential men and women around the world could learn.

Photo by Mark Rowland

CHOICES

Every day we have choices to make. We have to choose what to eat for breakfast for starters. Then on it goes: what to wear, which shoes to put on, who to eat lunch with, what to do after work, when to visit grandma, what to listen to on the radio, and which movie to watch. We have choices about where to live, where to send our children to school, what to become when we grow up, where to go on vacation. We can choose which bank to put our money into. We spend time wondering what color we should paint our house, which pet to buy, what sports to participate in, which diet to start. All the choices give us headaches and shoulder pains. Then we have to choose which medication to use.

Refugees are robbed of choice. They cannot choose which camp they want to live in. In the camp they do not get to choose where to put the shack that will serve as their home. They do not get to choose how big to make it. They do not get to choose what to eat or what to wear.

Many of them have just chosen to stay alive. Often they have chosen not to let the hardships they have faced make them bitter. Some of them have chosen to trust others even though so many have hurt them. The most amazing thing is to meet people who have chosen to forgive. And then, when common sense would tell them not to, they choose to continue trusting in God.

"IF YOU STEP ON ONE IT WILL BLOW
AND IT MAY KILL YOU
OR HURT YOU VERY BADLY."

LANDMINES

"Mommy, what are landmines?" I almost choked on the coffee I was drinking. Children six years of age ask how airplanes can fly and if dogs go to heaven. Most of them are not concerned with landmines. But this was the same child who, at the age of three, refused to play with another cute three-year-old because her friend had no idea what a refugee was. She did not like ignorant people.

I assured my daughter that we would never go where there were landmines. "They are dangerous objects that are hidden in the ground by the enemy. If you step on one it will blow up and it may kill you or hurt you very badly," I told her. I was glad I could tell her not to worry about these terrifying objects with confidence. I did not want her to have one more reason to wake up in the night with bad dreams. I did not want her to be afraid to go for walks in the mountains or in the jungle. I was also glad that she in fact was safe from landmines. How could I live if every time she went outside I was faced with the risk of her stepping on one?

Karen mothers in Burma cannot give the same assurance to their children. Instead they have to teach them how to stay away from landmines and how to live with the fear of them. When their children come and ask this question, they may answer: "It was a landmine that blew up and killed our neighbors' little boy when he was playing with a ball on the rice fields. You may also step on one and die, because they are well hidden and nobody can see them before they explode. When you step on one it is too late to run away."

THE OPRAH MAGAZINE

Sometimes I bring old magazines and calendars to the refugees. They love the bright pictures and usually cut out the pictures and hang them on the walls of their houses after the magazines have been thoroughly studied by many. One time I brought an old Oprah magazine.

"What is this?" a Karen man asked my friend. He was looking at an ad for NutraSweet. "It is fake sugar," my friend replied. "We use it instead of sugar so that we will not get fat." As the Karen man kept turning the pages I felt more and more awkward. Here he saw pictures of the latest in fashion, the new trends from the purse designers, articles on how to avoid having an affair and pictures of houses that put the word palace to shame. He saw ideas for dinners for people who were too busy to cook or too bored with chicken. He was introduced to ways to realize your dreams and ways to get confident enough to speak in public.

The world of Oprah looked like science fiction to these people as they waited for the rice that was cooking on top of a clay charcoal pot. People who would soon eat their simple meal of rice and fish paste before walking to the river to take a bath.

"Fake sugar. Who has ever heard of anything so silly?"

LEARNING STYLES

"Every child has the right to an education". This is one of the statements in the UN's declaration for children. It is so obvious. Why should we even have to make a point of letting people know this?

In the West we do not ask whether or not a child should go to school and learn. Here the questions are more complex. Such as: which phonics program should my child use? Where should I send my children to school? Public, private or at home? Is my child a visual or auditory learner? What is her learning style? What kind of shoes should she wear to school? Some days there are issues such as what to give them in their lunch sacks. How can we make them eat what they are given instead of feeding the trash can?

School or not? That has never been an issue. How we provide education, on the other hand, is a theme that people write their doctor's thesis on.

When displaced people live in hiding in the jungle, never knowing how much longer before the soldiers will find them and force them to flee again, they have different problems to consider than I do.

The children's learning style will not be discussed. But how to get some pieces of paper and some pencils to write with is an articulated concern. How to get the children to finish their lunch is not ever a problem. How to help them fight the fatigue they feel because they may not have eaten for a few days is a task harder than teaching them to read. The parents do not worry if the teacher is good enough for their children or if the school has the right ventilation system. Their only worry is whether their child will get an education at all and if the little school they built together with the other parents will be the first thing the soldiers burn to the ground if they are discovered.

THE CHILDREN'S LEARNING STYLE WILL NOT BE DISCUSSED. BUT HOW TO GET SOME PIECES OF PAPER AND SOME PENCILS TO WRITE WITH IS AN ARTICULATED CONCERN.

MEMORIES

April is so hot you just want to meditate yourself away. It feels like the earth was put into a box with no opening and then somebody turned the heater on high. It's Norway's January in reverse. April in Burma is as hot as January in Norway is cold. You have to want to live in order to survive it with your sanity intact.

That is the worst part about April. The good part is that there are mangoes! Yellow, juicy and sweet gifts from the modest looking trees that also house thousands of red ants. It is the month when the children in the villages take off all their clothes and spend long and untroubled days playing in the rivers. It is summer break from school. It is a time of carefree living. That is what every child in Burma ought to think of April.

Just like they ought to remember the rainy season as nightly outings hunting for frogs that will be dinner. Tiny raindrops make the cool air sparkle when the luckiest boy in the village turns on his flashlight to guide the rest of the group. Walking through mud and water is no burden when the reward will be fat, juicy frogs that taste excellent fried with chilies.

Then there is November in the mountains. November with the cold weather and long days spent harvesting rice on the fields. It's a joyous time for the children. All the villagers are harvesting together while singing songs that they only sing this time of the year, sharing stories and laughing. The children are running in the fields while trying to catch one of the many field rats. The first taste of the year's rice makes one dream of the New Year and all its possibilities. No rice is as soft and as fragrant as this one. Later some of it is stuffed into bamboo sticks and cooked over the fire. To make it a sweet treat some coconut milk and sugar is added. It is the taste of innocent childhood.

This is how it should be. Every child's good memory account ought to be full when he or she reaches adulthood. It may be memories of hunting for snakes in the bamboo brush or of cross-country skiing on snow that glitters. The memories of childhood could be of heart-shaped waffles on Valentine's Day or of fresh noodles with curry for a New Year celebration. The currency of the memories does not matter as long as the memories are good.

It's not that way though. Instead of a childhood filled with the joy of being alive, so many of Burma's children have been robbed. Feelings of disappointment, fear and pain have moved into the place where there was room for the good memories. The frog hunts have become races away from the enemy or a desperate search for food. The free feeling of harvest time has become a time of worrying about whether the enemy will come and burn all of it this year also. The New Year celebration is a desperate wish for a year to live in peace.

U2

I started listening to U2 and had a serious crush on Bono in 1986. That says something about my age. I ended up with a guy much better than Bono, but I still wonder if we really need any other music than U2's. It is a good question. I do see the benefit of Bach, Mozart, Miles Davis and an occasional Sarah McLachlan. But other than that?

There are 13 U2 albums. That gives us approximately 156 songs to listen to. That is a lot of songs. I've got music to guide my life.

Perhaps I was going over the edge when my kids watched U2 concerts instead of Sesame Street and I read Bono on Bono. He talked about getting closer to the melody that is in one's heart.

I have been thinking about that. It is about loving and knowing God, it is about being known by Him and accepted for who I am. It is about loving people the way He would love them. It is about fighting for justice and loving mercy. It is about grace.

How close am I to the melody in my heart?

I tend to be self-righteous. I think that I should be allowed to retire from being good one day soon. I have spent more than ten years of my life helping refugees for goodness sake! I should be able to start thinking about myself now. Can somebody else take over and let me go hiking in Norway?

I feel that I deserve a break. But that proves how badly I have missed the point, because it has nothing to do with: "Have I done enough yet?" It has to do with getting closer to the melody. It is about moving closer to God's heart. It is in pursuing the true purpose of my life that I will find the song that was written for me. The journey I am on with God will take me to His heart, and that is where I want to be. On the way there I will meet people who need me, whom it would be a sin to ignore.

Bono was a little concerned about becoming irrelevant and about not reaching his potential. Yeah, that could be a problem. How do you think that makes us feel, Bono? I did however take his words to heart and have decided to join him in the pursuit of potential. I will let grace be my guide.

Because grace finds goodness in everything. Grace finds beauty in everything. Grace makes beauty out of ugly things.

PERHAPS I WAS GOING OVER THE EDGE WHEN MY KIDS WATCHED U2 CONCERTS INSTEAD OF SESAME STREET AND I READ "BONO ON BONO".

CAMP LIFE

ONCE SETTLED IN
THE CAMP WITH A
ROOF OVER THEIR
HEADS, THEIR
NORMAL LIFE AS A
REFUGEE STARTS

They ran away from the land of their forefathers. They left nearly all their belongings when they fled. They spent days if not weeks hiding in an unwelcoming jungle. They saw loved ones die. They got sick. They suffered. Many starved.

Now they are in a camp. They made it here alive and are with each other at least. They may have lost everything they owned, everything they had lived for. Some have their spouses. Together they are going to make it through this difficult time. It may take them the rest of their years. They may not be free until they get to heaven. But they have each other. They can make it now.

If only it were that simple. Once settled in the camp with a roof over their heads, their normal life as a refugee starts: but where is the hope? I am of no use here. What shall our family eat? There are no hills on which to plant rice and grow vegetables. There are no mountains on which to graze the cattle. There is nothing to do.

Husbands whose lives have been shattered find their frustration building up. They do not know how to let it go. Some beat their wives and children. Domestic violence is the biggest social problem in a refugee camp.

My friend told me this as we were driving to a camp to visit our workers. "How can these gentle people be violent?" I asked myself. They are always smiling and look so friendly. Then I remembered what another friend who is a psychologist, told me: "When refugees have experienced trauma in their lives, they need a way to work through it. They need help to deal with the grief. If they don't, their pain will come out in destructive ways sooner or later." I understood.

CHILI AND STRESS

In my dreams I have a perfectly uncluttered house, the freezer is full of dinners that I always make the first day of the month, I buy all the Christmas presents by June and we have money left over at the end of each month.

OK, so this is just in my dreams. If I was to talk about real life it would be something like this: There are piles everywhere and I can't ever find a pair of scissors. I start thinking about what to eat for dinner about 17 minutes before it needs to be on the table. There is always more month than there is money. I just gave some Christmas presents to my family members, and it's already February. I need to clean the closets out before their contents come rolling out like an avalanche and bury us.

It seems impossible for me to have an organized life and to be the laidback mother who has time for everything and everyone. Instead I hurry everywhere. I cut cars off in traffic and give dirty looks to people who take too long and waste my time. I urge the kids to hurry up. We will be late. Late for what? Sometimes I do not know. We will just be late and that is bad.

I get a little stressed. I can't live up to my picture of perfect. I make my family suffer for my shortcomings and give myself shoulder pains.

Watching the refugees in the camps has helped me put things in perspective. It does not seem to matter that the closet is a mess in their houses. They do not have closets. They do not need one since they do not own enough things to put in one. They do not get irritated in traffic since they never get to leave the camp they live in. The thought of going for a drive anywhere, in whatever traffic, sounds like an exotic dream.

There are things that do matter though. Serving your guests a glass of water as soon as they come into your house. Offering your friends a comfortable place to sit. Preparing a meal for your visitors, no matter how little food you have in your house. Making people feel welcome in your presence.

Maybe I need to conform myself to the Karen model of hospitality and their value of relationships when I am together with my children, my husband, my co-workers and my friends. And not only that, but even when I am around people I do not even know, like that sales clerk who takes all the time in the world when I know that I need to get home to finish the chili for dinner. Maybe I should just forget about the mess and invite more people over to help eat the chili.

I GET A LITTLE STRESSED. I CAN'T LIVE UP TO MY PICTURE OF PERFECT.

"I SEE A PICTURE OF A LITTLE BOY HAVING

SCHOOL IN THE JUNGLE

AND I SEE A CHILD NO DIFFERENT THAN MINE.

THE CELLS THAT MAKE HIS BODY ARE MUCH THE SAME

AS THE CELLS IN MY CHILDREN'S BODIES."

FIRST DAY OF SCHOOL

It was the first day of school. Naomi, our middle daughter, was going to start first grade. We had taken out her brand new clothes and placed them neatly on her bed the night before. The backpack was ready to be picked up in the hallway. Two days ago we had gone to the hairdresser and gotten a haircut that had satisfied the little first grader. She had a very difficult time going to sleep the night before. Wonder who the teacher will be? Wonder if I will make any friends? Wonder if my shoes are cool enough? Dad made sure the camera was ready to take pictures of everything, starting with the family piled in the hallway, all of us trying to get out of the door at the same time. He made sure he got pictures of the class, the desk, the teacher, the playground, the hooks where they had hung their jackets and the blackboard with Welcome written on it.

The first day of school. It was a happy day for Naomi. She came home with new books and pencils as sharp as the hot dog stick she had recently made. In her backpack was a box of unused crayons and an eraser that still had neither bite marks nor any black stains from too much use. She had made new friends. She was in love with her teacher.

Inside the jungle of Burma a little boy Naomi's age was also going to start school. His parents were equally excited that their boy was going to have the opportunity to learn to read and write. Not only that, he was also going to have something to fill his idle days with. He would be playing with friends and learning useful skills for his future. He had no new clothes for the special day.

He did not even have shoes to wear. But his love for his teacher could be compared to Naomi's love for hers. The smile on his face after writing the first few letters on the blackboard that the teacher let the children take turns using, was no less proud than Naomi's smile as she showed her teacher the first few pages of her workbook.

There are times, I have to admit, that I think of the refugees in terms of us and them. Sometimes doing that helps me cope with the stories I hear about them. It becomes a way to distance myself from the realities of lives lived in poverty, fear and pain. If I can think about them as a mass of people far removed from me, I can convince myself that maybe their pain is not as real as mine. When I distance myself from them and start thinking of them as a large group of people rather than individuals I find excuses for my own lack of involvement.

But then I see a picture of a little boy having school in the jungle and he somehow makes me see him as a child no different than mine. The cells that make up his body are much the same as the cells in my own children's bodies. The heart that pumps his blood is made in the same amazing way as the hearts of my own daughters. His brain has been wired with millions of little brain wires, making him more amazing than the most wonderful computer. He feels happiness, fear, sadness, cold, hunger and pain exactly the same way we do.

It bugs me. Because then the people come so close. Then I feel like I can't just ignore what they feel. Then I can't just ignore the pain. I start to almost feel it myself.

I think it should bug me. Not to fill me with guilt and hopelessness, but to wake up my heart. I need to feel my heart and sense the pain so the people we are helping are not simply numbers on pages and faces with no names. I need to think of them as people who are as excited about the first day of school as my little girl.

Photo by Steve Gumaer

NAW LAH DAH

I noticed her right away in the crowd of people whose eyes were all on us.

We were in a cramped bamboo house in a refugee camp. The house was the home of over 20 teenagers who had left their homes to come and live in a refugee camp. But the person I noticed most among them was a young mother with a toddler in her arms. Her face was open and eager. Her eyes held in them the kind of passion that could change the world. At least it could change lives.

"Hello, my name is Naw Lah Dah," she smiled at me under a purple baseball cap with an English flag on it. "I am very pleased to meet you. I really enjoyed your performance." Her English was perfect; only a slight accent revealed that Karen was her mother tongue. I asked her to join me as we walked back to our house on the other side of the camp.

During our walk it amazed me to find out how much we had in common. She had three children the same age as mine. We shared a lot of the same interests and I felt that this was a woman that could have become my best friend if we had grown up together. "How about your husband?" I asked. "He stepped on a landmine some years ago and lost his leg. He used to be active fighting for the Karen people's freedom. Now he mostly sits at home." She wasn't complaining, just telling me the facts. As she told me this we passed her house. It was not much different from all the other small bamboo houses in the camp. Nothing more than a hut that had a floor to sleep on.

I heard about her desire to educate the youth in the camp. Enthusiasm laced her voice as she talked about health care. This was a woman who could have led a nation, who could have inspired an army, who could have given knowledge and wisdom to scientists had she had the opportunity. This was a woman who could have reached a place in society where people would have come to her for advice, who would have been paid her for opinions.

Yet, there she was, walking barefoot through a refugee camp, wearing one of her two shirts and proudly wearing her brand new cap. Her influence would most likely not reach beyond the boundaries of the camp she lives in. Perhaps she will never leave the camp to go back to her home country. Her dreams will probably never come true.

I left feeling guilty about my abundant life, my privileges, and all my opportunities. Why were our lives so different? Why did I have so much and she nothing? I could not find an answer. The only thing I knew was that it felt wrong.

PRIVACY OF THIN WALLS

Houses built of bamboo. Thin walls that allow not only for the wind to blow through, but also for all the sounds to freely travel in and out. I wonder if they ever argue or gossip about their neighbors. Do they just get used to always hearing everything that the people next door talk about? Do they go on pretending they didn't hear anything? Or maybe they just whisper? Do they say insensitive and impulsive things to their kids when they get annoyed with them? It would be hard for me to hold my tongue if it was my home.

I value my privacy. I like to close the curtains at night so that nobody can see inside my own little world. I like to yell at my kids when nobody hears it. I want the romantic nights with my husband to be only for the two of us.

I like to lock the door at night when I go to bed so nobody can come inside while I am sleeping. I would not feel safe if all that was between me and the rest of the world were some thin walls of bamboo, if that.

EDUCATIONAL TOYS

Toys seem to consume and clutter my life. People who see my house on any average Tuesday may wonder if they've walked into a storage room for a toy store, or into the home of a family whose children have too much influence on its interior design.

I try to hide the evidence of our disgusting abundance in decorative baskets and on custom-made shelves. But no matter how hard I try, it seems like in every room you will either step on some Lego pieces, walk into a Polly Pocket tea party, observe a Barbie fashion show, wake up a Baby Born who is sleeping in her own Port-a-crib, slide on some pretty princess dress-up clothes or stumble over an American Girl doll and all her old-fashioned outfits. You may find it hard to find room for your coffee cup on the table that has piles of art supplies and a collection of puzzles and games. The couch has a small library on it. If you want to sit down, you had better use one of the brightly colored pillows the children use to build play forts.

Like most mothers I got tricked into thinking that all the toys I got for my children were educational. When we had our first baby, we spent our money on the right kind of rattles and baby displays. We kept the trend up into the toddler years by giving them sturdy wooden toys to develop motor skills and help their brains grow fast. Our pre-schoolers got puzzles and clay, along with their first dolls. This was to stimulate creativity. Our elementary school daughters were given American Girl dolls to learn history. But do we really need it all in order to raise a child who is good at math or who will aspire to become an artist? Probably not.

We have too much. If I took all the toys my three daughters own to Peh Lu's orphanage with 60 children in it, it would be more toys than all those children combined have seen their entire life. Could it be that Hello Kitty and Nutcracker Barbie would benefit from a cross-cultural experience? Should I relocate them to a refugee camp? Refugee Barbie? That is an idea I personally find very appealing.

I TRY TO HIDE THE
EVIDENCE OF OUR
DISGUSTING ABUNDANCE
IN DECORATIVE BASKETS
AND ON CUSTOM MADE
SHELVES.

CHEATERS

Do you remember playing Monopoly as a child and cheating in order to win? Remember that bad feeling? Winning by using dishonest means stinks, and I always thought that everybody else smelled it. And even if they didn't, it was bad enough to make me feel sick. Remember taking credit for something somebody else did or said? No matter how small, it still made me feel like a twerp to realize I made myself look good by using other people.

Don't you wonder what it looks like inside a dictator's head? What are the thoughts that control the actions of leaders of a military regime that has come to power by using the most dishonest means? Is there a voice there that says: You cheated. You are still cheating. You are stealing. You are a coward.

The still voice has probably been silenced, their actions justified to themselves and the people they surround themselves with. They have lied so much that they believe it themselves.

What do they think about when they get up in the morning and go to eat their breakfast? Do they sit down with their OJ and boiled rice and count how many soldiers they have to keep busy today? Do they put on their freshly ironed brown polyester uniforms while thinking about how many children's deaths they are responsible for? Do they avoid looking in the direction of the house where Aung San Suu Kyi has been under house arrest for more than 11 years because it will remind them that they cheated? They are pretending they won the Monopoly game, but she did.

How do they justify their riches to themselves when just outside their kitchen window live some of the world's poorest people? Do they enjoy the rides in their Mercedeses or does it leave a yucky feeling in the stomach? their stomachs?

Are they worried? I was always worried that I would get caught if I cheated. Because one always does. I think the rulers in Burma know that too. That is why I think that behind the dark glasses, inside the uniforms full of shiny medals, under the wide brimmed hats, behind faces that radiate arrogance and hunger for power, are men who are scared and paranoid. They know just like we do that the their day of justice will come. On that day they will be held accountable for what they did to a whole country over many generations.

I find strange comfort in God's word about the wicked leaders of Burma: *"The wicked plots against the just, and gnashes at him with his teeth. The Lord laughs at him, for he sees that his day is coming. The wicked have drawn the sword and have bent their bow, to cast down the poor and needy, to slay those who are of upright conduct. Their sword shall enter their own heart, and their bows shall be broken. A little that a righteous man has is better than the riches of the many wicked. For the arms of the wicked shall be broken, but the Lord upholds the righteous."* Ps.37: 12-17 (NIV)

SOLDIERS

The chocolate brown river made its way south and was oblivious to the fact that it served as the border between two nations. Burma on one side, Thailand on the other. We felt safe in the long, narrow boat that was going to take us to a place we had only heard about. I knew that behind the green mountains, only a few miles away, people were running for their lives. But here everything seemed so peaceful. A bright blue bird caught my attention. Like a cheerful spot of color it danced across the sky above us. It made me feel hopeful in a strange way.

Suddenly I noticed something else: Soldiers. They were on the Burmese side of the border, and they had guns. With unfriendly waves and loud commands that I understood, even though I do not speak one word of Burmese, we were summoned towards the shore. I looked around to see if I could see a trace of fear in the faces of our Karen friends. But their faces revealed about as much as a rock would have. One of them gave me some important information though: These are SPDC soldiers (soldiers from the Burmese Army). That did not make me any less scared.

While the soldiers continued to wave at us, the boat driver brought us as close as possible to the Thai side. The danger we were in did not last long, and it was never very serious, I found out later.

For me this was the first time to see the armed men who have destroyed so much of Burma. For a few minutes I felt a tiny bit of the fear that people must feel when they see soldiers approaching their villages. I understood a little of the fear a woman must feel when she runs into a soldier on her way home from a rice field.

I felt fear for some minutes. For the people of Burma the fear is a constant part of their lives.

I LOOKED AROUND TO SEE IF I COULD SEE A TRACE OF FEAR IN THE FACES OF OUR KAREN FRIENDS. BUT THEIR FACES REVEALED ABOUT AS MUCH AS A ROCK WOULD HAVE.

DREAMS

Listening to a copy of ABBA's Greatest Hits that we bought on the Thai-Burma border crossing, I told my girls about my dream of becoming a pop star when I was their age. My best friend and I would pretend we were Frida and Agnetha, who were taking the world by storm whilst singing Mama Mia. We had dreamed of fame and money, of diamond necklaces and unlimited credit at the toy store in town. My daughters laughed at me. They have heard me sing and know why the breakthrough never came!

I have had other dreams too. Some of them have come through, others have not. I am glad I never got the castle with all the pastel colors— pink couches and curtains would have eventually left me nauseous. I never did wake up one morning and find I was suddenly an amazing ballerina. But a handsome prince did actually come for me. He did not ride on a white horse nor did he carry a shining sword to kill the enemy. He took me rock climbing and he does tell me he thinks I am beautiful even after the hairdresser has messed up terribly.

We all have dreams and we should never let them die. Doesn't hope die along with our dreams?

I have seen people in the refugee camps who have stopped dreaming and lost their hope. They have given up on life. They do not have any reason to keep living. Then I have met others who believe in a future that holds their dreams. They study for an education, they learn skills that can be useful, and they fight battles for the freedom of their people and for the right to live. They risk their lives for something they believe in.

A military dictatorship can kill its people, take away their belongings and their dignity. But it is only when it takes away the ability to dream that the people really die.

WE ALL HAVE DREAMS AND WE SHOULD NEVER LET THEM DIE. DOESN'T HOPE DIE ALONG WITH OUR DREAMS?

"MY LIFE HAS PEOPLE AS ITS MAIN INGREDIENT

AND STILL THERE ARE TIMES

WHEN I FIND THAT I AM LONELY.

I AM AN OXYMORON."

NOT ALONE, BUT LONELY

Some days I go to the bathroom to be alone. I know that there are a few others in the world who have this habit. It is mostly mothers of young children. I lock the door and bring a book or a magazine and sit there until I hear something fall in the next room with a loud bang, or until the screams are loud enough to alarm the neighbors.

My personality profile says I am an introvert. I need time alone to get recharged. Since I do this in the bathroom, it is rather obvious that I am not often fully recharged. It would be easier if I was like my iPod. Plug me in to the computer for a while and I will play any tune you want.

Yes, being alone is a luxury. If it is not my kids, it is all the other people. They are everywhere. I often find them in my house for dinner. They are at the meetings I attend; they smile and say hi when I go jogging; they are even at my favorite coffee shop occupying my chosen table.

My life has people as its main ingredient and still there are times when I find that I am lonely. I am an oxymoron.

Very few people know who I am behind the hippie necklaces and the red lipstick. I can bake delicious bread and knit patterns that will impress my math teacher, but do I tell my friends about my fears and shortcomings? I often don't. It could be risky. Maybe they would like me less if they found out who I really am. The fear of rejection has roots that are difficult to pull completely out.

It is easy to forget that living in a refugee camp with as many as 30,000 others, where the houses are so close that you can reach over and touch your neighbor, people can also be lonely at the same time as they long to be alone. I do not know if they hide in the bathroom to get solitude. It is unlikely since there are community latrines. But I think it is safe to assume that although they can't even pick their noses in private, many are lonely and desperate for intimate fellowship.

As I am thinking about this I feel that I have things to be thankful for. When the noise around me is so overwhelming that I think I may join the screaming choir, I do have a clean quiet bathroom to retreat to. Many people do not have that luxury.

And when loneliness attacks me, I can choose to stay in my arrogant self-pity afraid to disclose who I really am, or I can move away from it, assured that even though rejection may come, it will never take away the love God has for me. By choosing to believe God's truth about who I am, I can minister to the refugees with confidence and love.

IN THE MORNING

I pick up my Bible in the morning and read what God wants to say to me through His word. It challenges me, inspires me, and encourages me. Then I choose one of the many books I own, written by people who have insightful things to say about God, His word and my life in this world. Again I am challenged and changed by what I read. It is a treasure that I need. It wakes me up on the inside. It leaves me desiring to get closer to God and to reach for more of Him in my life.

I wonder what I would do if I did not have the Bible, or only parts of it. What if there were no Christian books that I could go to for answers and inspiration? What if I came to a part of Scripture that I did not understand, but there was nobody I could go to who could help me figure it out, no book I could look the problem up in, no web site I could search? How would my faith be if the last sermon I heard from somebody was a few years ago?

What if there were no more church services to attend since the pastor had been executed publicly for refusing to renounce his faith? What if the only time I got to fellowship with fellow believers was in a secret hiding place deep in the jungle where we could only speak in hushed voices? What would that do to my faith?

Such is the faith journey of many of the Karen people I know.

GENEROUS

The art of generosity is something I admire in people and strive to be proficient at myself. One time I learned a lesson about generosity that I will never forget.

We were in a hill tribe village so far away that it made us confident we had fulfilled Jesus' calling to go to the ends of the world. In a world that consisted of only 50 families, their livestock and rice paddies, the mountains around them and the sky above them, we had become the guests of honor. We were seated on the village's only five chairs, in a hot and humid room that served as the community hall. It had been decorated with fresh flowers from the jungle close by. All around us were the faces of curious villagers. The adults sat on the floor in front of us and felt no embarrassment by the fact that they were staring at us, pointing at us and laughing at us. While studying us, the monkeys in the zoo, they eagerly picked their noses and chewed their tobacco. Spitting was as natural as breathing. Sometimes it ended up between the cracks in the floor, hitting poor chickens on the head. Other times the aim was bad, so the evidence of humans was left like wet mini puddles on the floor.

To our surprise, one of the leaders in the village stood up and told everybody gathered that this ceremony was in honor of us. The villagers had come to thank us for the work we had been doing for them for ten years. We knew that it had not been ten years, but who could blame them for losing track of time in a place where nobody owned a watch and the only calendar that could be found was from 1979?

While the children sang songs they had practiced for us to hear I was touched. Their clothes were so dirty. On one of the girls I could see a shirt that once had belonged to my daughter. After the songs, the adults came forward one by one and shared words of thanks for us. All I could think about was how much they had given *us*.

In the end we were told that now the villagers were going to present us with gifts. The people in front of us were some of the poorest in the world. What were they going to give us, and how could we receive it from them?

I will never forget the humbling feeling of sitting before these villagers while one after the other they came forward and gave us of their crop. We got bags of rice they had just harvested, pumpkins straight from the field, bananas picked from their trees, a handmade broom and cloth that they had woven themselves. I knew they needed what they gave us more than we did. Still I don't think I have ever received nicer gifts.

The villagers in this village taught us something that day. They taught us about thankfulness and generosity. They did not give of their abundance. They gave when they had nothing. They showed their gratitude not only with a nod and a smile. Their thankfulness was expressed from their hearts. I wonder if I will ever be able to explain to them that in my eyes they are greater people than I am. In my eyes they have given us something more valuable than we can ever give them.

Next time I go to the village, they will probably still sit up in their bamboo houses, looking down at us while they are smoking their pipes, nursing a baby or making a tool. Their lifestyle is so simple. We complicated people should watch and learn.

THE VILLAGERS IN THIS VILLAGE TAUGHT US SOMETHING THAT DAY. THEY TAUGHT US ABOUT THANKFULNESS AND GENEROSITY. THEY DID NOT GIVE OF THEIR ABUNDANCE. THEY GAVE WHEN THEY HAD ALMOST NOTHING.

WHY IS THERE SUFFERING IN BURMA?

"Burma, a country of 50 million people, is ruled by fear. A military machine of 500,000 soldiers denies the whole nation its most basic rights." (Burma Campaign, UK)

The nation of Burma (now called Myanmar) has been in a civil war for more than 50 years. In 1988, after decades under a brutal military regime, a widespread movement for democracy culminated in the massacre of thousands of peaceful demonstrators. The military dictatorship bowed to intense pressure and finally held elections in 1990. The National League for Democracy Party won over 80% of the votes. However, the results were ignored, and leaders of the opposition imprisoned, including Aung San Suu Kyi, the NLD party leader who was later awarded the Nobel Peace Prize. (FBR)

Few understand the Burmese military junta's cruel intentions better than the various ethnic groups in the country. To gain control over land and valuable resources, the Burmese Army has invaded village after village. New people are constantly joining the estimated 1.5 million who are already hiding in the jungles.

The Burma Army (who call themselves the State Peace & Development Council-SPDC) goes systematically from village to village, burning houses, destroying belongings and placing landmines around villages. People are forced to leave their homes, and if they don't run fast enough they risk getting shot.

The goal of the SPDC is to cut civilians off from their livelihood and create an atmosphere of fear and terror. Consequently they cut the resistance groups from the support they need. To feed their men, the SPDC demands that civilians give them their rice and livestock, as well as products they have for sale in their markets. Those who do not submit to their demands are severely punished.

When villagers are in the way of the government's building projects, they are forced to relocate and are given no compensation. Additionally, civilians are used as human porters, slaves and mine sweepers. Rape is a commonly used weapon against women and girls. Torture and extra-judicial killings are often reported.

For the displaced people who are hiding in the jungle the situation is desperate. They do not have enough food or clean water. They have no sanitation facilities. They get sick and have no medicine. Malaria is common, especially among the children. They are malnourished and dehydrated; they contract dysentery and stomach diseases. For the women the situation is particularly difficult, especially for those who are pregnant. Many give birth prematurely or miscarry.

The greatest needs are for safety, food, medicine and help to continue the children's schooling even while they live in hiding. More than anything else they simply want to go back to their homes and live in peace on the land they have occupied for many generations.

WHAT ABOUT PARTNERS?

Social activism was never just a word for me. It was part of who I was. It described me. Hippie clothes. Peace buttons on my jackets. Bring justice to the proletariat! It started by wanting to send apples to the poor children in Africa when I was 4, and escalated into rallies on the streets demanding that the Robin Hood ideology be applied to the world: Take from the rich and give to the poor.

However, when my husband and I were invited to visit refugees on the Thai-Burma border in 1994, I was a bit weary of trying to change the world. My simple solutions did not appear to work. Nobody even seemed interested in hearing them.

So it wasn't activism that led me to Sho Klo refugee camp. It was the promise of adventure.

I got adventure, and I got something else as well. What happened on that first meeting with the Karen refugees from Burma changed our lives forever. Sitting on stained bamboo floors while drinking sweet coffee from dusty coffee cups, listening to stories of broken lives and broken dreams, but also of courage and hope, hearing about abuse, torture and death, but also about love, faith and music woke something up inside us. We weren't drawn to an ideology or a new doctrine that we could convert people to. We were drawn to the people. We were drawn to their stories and to their lives. We started thinking of them as our friends rather than people in need. Their faces, their smiles, their hospitality, the way they dressed, cooked, took showers and carried their baskets on their heads all helped pull us into their lives.

That was the beginning of Partners. Because as we were getting ready to go home, we realized we would never be the same. We could not leave our new friends with a promise to pray for them and the encouragement of Jesus' love, and then do nothing else. We had to get involved. To do anything else would be to ignore the voice of God.

Living on $500 a month did not give room for much extravagance, but we were able to give some. Backpacks were filled with what supplies we could get every month. Traveling on non air-conditioned buses and the back of trucks to deliver the goods seemed like a small sacrifice. "But whoever has this world's goods, and sees his brother in need, and shuts up his heart from him, how does the love of God abide in him? My little children, let us not love in word or in tongue, but in deed and truth." 1.John 3:17-18. The challenge couldn't be more black and white!

Partners has gone from being two slightly disillusioned young people with a desire to help to an organization with a name, a logo, a budget and boards in many countries (USA, Canada, Australia, UK and Norway). What is more, Partners is able to help thousands of refugees every year. Our work is mostly focused on the 1.5 million internally displaced people (IDPs) who are hiding in the jungles and mountains of Burma. Our focus has been the needs of orphans and the other children of war, medical aid and training as well as leadership training.

Photo by Trond Hattrem

"YOU CAN'T JUST PRAY FOR 1.5 MILLION REFUGEES,
TELL THEM THAT JESUS LOVES THEM,
AND THEN LEAVE THEM HUNGRY, WITHOUT CLOTHES, AND SICK;
YOU HAVE TO DO SOMETHING FOR THEM
TO DEMONSTRATE THE HEART AND TRUTH BEHIND THE PRAYER"

(STEVE GUMAER)

THABLUU (THANKS)

This book has happened over many years. It wasn't even supposed to become a book. I just wrote thoughts down as they fell into my head. Then we put some of my writing in our magazine and people wrote and said they liked it. Some people even taped it to their refrigerator. Notes of encouragement can get anybody to write. That's what happened to me.

There is, however, no way at all that I would have thought a thought so crazy as to publish a book. The person who made that happen is Steve. Since the day we met he has believed in me, and made me do things I never thought I could do, like driving a car for example. Over the years he has read almost everything I have written and never once has he told me it was rubbish. Instead he has encouraged me to keep writing. He has made it sound like I have a talent. I have believed him and, full of ideas of literary fame, I have kept writing and writing about refugee life. It is a gift to have a husband and a best friend who makes sure his wife publishes a book.

I could not have written the stories I have without my three daughters, Elise, Naomi and Kristin. Without them in my life there simply would not be much to write about. They are my greatest joys and challenges. They are also my cheerleaders who listen to what I write and tell me it sounds better than anything they could have written.

Brent's photos speak. I am honored to be able to use the photos of a person whom I consider one of the best photographers in Thailand. Even if there were no words in this book, Brent's beautiful images would still tell a story of the lives of the refugees.

There are other people who deserve to have their names mentioned here: my great and faithful friend Ruth who took the time to read through the manuscript with all its flaws and gave me her honest opinion about it. She used so much red ink that I think she had to buy a new pen. Only a good friend would do that.

Craig and Kara landed in our lives and we can't figure out why we deserve them. We have warned them about the dangers of interacting with us too much, but they seem to like a life of unpredictable adventure. I also told them that they could throw my book in the trash can, but they didn't. Instead they gave valuable feedback and comments.

Dave and Karen. I will never forget the lunch we had when Karen got to eat liver pate on her bread and Dave told us not to let fear or the desire for comfort guide our lives. Neither will I forget that they challenged me to keep writing. You have to understand, any advice from D&K is not taken with a grain of salt in this camp.

Another gift was meeting Michael LaRocca. Now I can say that a professional editor has read through my work. He has helped me with compound words, commas and other grammar stuff that I did not know mattered. Not only that, but his great sense of humor has made me laugh and his encouragements have –encouraged me.

Then there is my hero Cathrin who helped me with the layout of the book. Everything Cat does looks superb. Juliet: I was honored that you read the manuscript and gave us your feedback. Val: you are amazing as usual.

God has given me a life worth living. He has given me a purpose and a calling. He has led me into things that only He could have dreamed up. I am blessed to be a follower of Jesus.

* * * *